The Ultimate Interview Guidebook

The only interview guide you will ever need in your life

AMARPREET SINGH

info@thethoughtflame.com

www.thethoughtflame.com

Table of Contents

Introduction

Whenever you have an interview set up at a potential job, one of the many things that may be running through your mind is that you are the ideal candidate for the position. While that may be true, the person who will be interviewing you may not be thinking along the same lines. Remember, when it comes to the interviewing process there are a variety of things that you should be considering such as what your answer will be for a certain interview question or what you will need to wear during the interview.

If I were to tell you the variety of things that you should and should not do during an interview, this book would be hundreds of pages long. However, in this eBook I will teach you everything that you need to know in order to ace your interview and to get the job of your dreams. You will learn everything you need to know from the kind of questions you need to practice answering for to what clothes you should wear on interview day.

Chapter One: Why it is Important to Ace Your Interview and What Is Going Through your Interviewer's Mind

In an interview, the way that you act and hold yourself can mean the difference between nailing the interview or failing it and continuing your job search. There have been a variety of studies that have been conducted on the importance of body language during the interview process and it has been found that nearly 55% of body language that is used causes those who you are talking to respond to whatever it is that you are saying. On the other hand when you are only using your voice to communicate, only 7% of verbal language causes those around you to respond in kind.

Believe it or not, nonverbal communication is just as important during the interview process as any other form of language. You need to keep in mind that your body language will impact the overall outcome of your interview so it is important that the moment you walk in through the door your body language skills are up to par. As I said, it can mean the difference between wowing your interviewers or turning them off to the idea of you becoming a member of their company.

Why Nonverbal Communication Is Important

Whenever you have an interview, the way that you present yourself and what your body language says about you is key to your own success. If you walk into your interview chewing a stick of gum or smelling like an ashtray, you will already have one strike counted against you. If you wear too much perfume or cologne that too won't help you. If you walk in not dressed for the job that you want and are just wearing a pair of ripped jeans or some scuffed up shoes, you will take another strike against you. Talking on your cell phone or listening to music won't help either.

Remember, the more professional that you look, the better your interview will go and the more professional your interviewers will see you as. Before you leave your home for your interview, make sure that you not only dressed as professionally as possible, but that you appear to be well groomed and haven't overdone it on both your perfume or your makeup. You need to keep in mind that you are not just going to meet with one person during your interview. More than one person will see you once you walk through the door and you need to ensure that you impress every single person that you see.

There are a variety of different things that you need to bring to your interview with you as well as a variety of things that would be best if they are left at home.

Things You Should Bring To Your Interview

1. Pen and a Notepad-the reason that you want to bring this is because not only is it important to take notes during your interview, but it will show your interviewers that you are truly interested in the job.

2. Breath Mint-while this item may seem ridiculous, it is nonetheless important. You don't want to come into an interview while a breath reeking of garlic. It is best to be safe than sorry.

3. A Portfolio-you will need to have something to hold your important documents such as a resume, reference list and cover letter. All of

these items should be printed on high quality paper to impress your interviewers.

Things That You Should Not Bring To Your Interview

1. Cell Phone and iPod-if there is anything that will turn off your interviewers and will leave them thinking that you are a unprofessional person it is a cell phone and an iPod. Even if you are waiting to be called for your interview you should never play with your cell phone or listen to music on your iPod. It is best to simply wait patiently and attentively.

2. A Pack of Cigarettes or a Pack of Gum-if an interviewer sees a pack of cigarettes in your pocket, they will know you are a smoker and most likely never hire you for the position you are applying for.

3. A Cup Of Coffee-this is highly unprofessional and will not impress your interviewers one bit. Simply wait to have coffee after your interview.

What To Do When You Are Waiting To Be Called For Your Interview

You would be surprised that just by the way you sit in a lobby when you are waiting to be called for an interview can actually impact the way the interview goes whether it is that you walk away with a new job or if you continue your job search. It all comes down to your attitude, which needs to be both pleasant and friendly, but should not be overdone. If you need to wait for some time, then wait and do so patiently and calmly.

Once you are called don't forget to greet your interviewer in a friendly manner and shake their hand firmly but not so much so. There are a few nonverbal communication acts that you should do during your interview. Here is a list that you should follow to a T if you wish to nail your dream job.

1. Make sure that you make consistent eye contact throughout the entire interview process. However, do not simply stare down the interviewer or else you will most likely scare them off. The key is to only make contact a few seconds at a time.

2. Make sure that you nod and smile during the appropriate times during the interview. Make sure that you don't overdo it or else the interviewer will not think you actually understand what it is they are saying.

3. Keep track of the tone of your voice. Don't speak too loudly or too quiet. Keep your tone even throughout the entire process.

4. Keep a straight posture. Don't slouch in your seat. This will make your interviewer think that you are listening intently and are actually focused on whatever it is they are saying.

5. Relax. There is no need to stress out over an interview, no matter how important it is. The

worst answer you can hear from your interviewer is that they have no interest in hiring you. If that happens then simply continue your job search.

6. Make sure that you pay attention the entire time and make sure that you appear both attentive and interested in what the interviewer is saying.

7. Do not interrupt your interview. This is simply rude and can affect how the rest of your interview goes.

8. If you do not know what to do with your hands then try holding a pen in your hand and have your notepad in the other hand. This will not only help you from becoming distracted and playing with your hands during the interview but it will also help to make you look professional to your interviewer. It is important that if you are the type of person who speaks with your hands to control your hand

movements and do not let them fly all over the place.

Nonverbal communication is important but so are your verbal communication skills. It is important that you keep your manners in mind and make sure that you thank your interviewer at the end of your interview for taking the time to see and meet with you. Whatever you do, do not use slang when you are talking. Talk using proper English and make sure that you speak as clearly as you can.

Remember, the first image that your interviewer has of you is the moment they first meet you so it is important that you grab their attention right from the get-go. If your interviewer first lays their eyes on you and sees a slouchy and messy person, it is going to matter how you answer whatever interview questions that are thrown at you. You won't get the job. It is important to practice for your interview beforehand and make sure that you work on your nonverbal communication skills before the actual interview.

What Is Going Through Your Interviewer's Mind

To many, an interviewer is one of the scariest people they will ever encounter. However, they are people just as scared of meeting you as well. Have you ever wondered what is going through your interviewers mind during an actual interview? Well, you would not be the only one. Here is a list of 10 different things that you may have never realized that is going through your interviewer's mind.

1. They Only Want To Find The Best Person For The Position-interviews are stressful. There is no denying it. It is easy for both parties involved to view each other as an adversary rather than what is important: filling the position with the perfect person. In every interview, believe it or not the interviewer comes into the room and hopes that you will be the right person they are looking for. After all, there is a position that needs to be filled and that is just sitting there unoccupied and affecting how their company is running. The main fear of any interviewer is that they will fill the position they need with someone who will not excel in it.

2. Interviewers Are Busy People-the one thing that you need to realize is that interviewers are one of the busiest people on the planet. It is completely normal for them to not have enough time that they can take out of their busy day in order to follow up with prospective candidates for the position they are hiring for. Interviewers that are dedicated to finding the perfect person will eventually get back to the people they interview, but sometimes it takes longer than they both expected or liked. It is also usual for those who call back their interviewers on the status of the position will often not have their questions answered. This is nothing person, it is just that the interviewer is extremely busy.

3. The Human Resources Department Run The Show When It Comes To Interviews-it is not uncommon for many human resources department to control every aspect of the hiring process down to the interview. The way that you can spot a company with a human resources department is if you encounter an interviewer who never deviates from the same interview questions or if you have an interviewer that will not comment or give you feedback on how the interview went.

4. Many Interviewers Are Simply Afraid of Hiring The Wrong Person-let's face it. If you are hired for a computer programming job but have no experience with using computers or how to even program a computer using C++ or HTML, you will not last long at your job. Interviewers know this and they know the high cost of hiring the wrong person for the position they need filled: disruption of the daily work life, months of unnecessary written warnings, the need to fire the person eventually in the future and loss of money for paying someone to not do the job correctly. That is why the interview process is crucially important because interviewers need to hire the right person right off of the bat.

5. The Need To Hire Someone That Every Employee In The Company Will Get Along With-you need to keep in mind that hiring someone for a certain position isn't just about hiring someone to get the job done. It is also about hiring the right person that everybody in the company will get along with.

Interviewers know that whoever they hire will be a person they will spend a lot of time with over the next couple of months or even the next couple of years. In the end it doesn't come down to how skilled the person is, it comes down to their overall attitude and their demeanor with the other people they work with. There is nothing worse than working with someone who is constantly whining or constantly arguing with their fellow employees.

6. They Need To Figure Out How Tough You Are Going To Be To Manage-smart interviewers will ask you a ton of questions not to see how you answer them, but to figure out if you are going to be worth managing in the long run. They need to figure out if you will need every micro-detail of an assignment when you are given it, if you are going to be a person who will never give helpful insight on what they think about a person or a project or if you are going to be an employee that needs their hand held during the entire workday. Interviewers are always on the lookout for how their potential employees are going to be once they are hired and are on the lookout for red flags that indicate that a person will not be the best person to work for their company.

7. They Need You To Tell Them Why They Should Hire You To Fill Their Position-interviewers have a tough time judging a person by themselves. Sometimes they need help in figuring out if you will be an ideal candidate for their position. You help them out greatly by answering questions related to real-life situations you have found yourself in and examples of the kind of work you have done before.

8. Know That An Interviewer Will Most Likely Never Tell You What They Really Think-in an interview have you ever noticed how an interviewer will sit back and nod their head occasionally as if they agree with whatever it is that you are saying? The truth is what they are doing is analyzing every word that you say whether it is that you are bad mouthing the owner of the company you previously worked for or if you said something that is a deal breaker for them. However, the chance of you hearing what they are thinking is slim to none so don't look for the interviewer to express what they feel about you until they call you back, if they even do.

9. During The Interview They Are Wondering What You Are Not Telling Them-it is no secret that those interviewing for a position aren't always honest about what they say. Even if the candidate is being as honest as possible the interviewer doesn't know that and they are sitting back and looking at you simply wondering if you are leaving a few details out, whether they are minor or major details.

10. They Hate Saying No To People-one of the few things that an interviewer absolutely hates to do is to reject a potential candidate. They hate it so much in fact that a few interviews will not even call the people back to let them they are not chosen for the position. Even though it is really unfair and rude to potential candidates, they know this and they also know that many people depended on this job or may have really wanted it. The fact is they hate it and you as a candidate should keep that in mind.

There are a variety of different factors that you need to consider when going into your interview such as knowing exactly how your nonverbal body language will impact the outcome of your interview and exactly what it is your interviewer is thinking throughout the entire process. Knowing exactly how you need to carry yourself the moment you walk in through the door and what it is your interviewer is thinking can either make or break a potential hiring in the long run and it can help you to successfully nail your next job interview.

Chapter Two: What To Do In Any Interview and A Few Helpful Tips To Nailing It

Whether you know it or not, having an interview scheduled is something worthy of celebration. Why? It is because all of the countless hours you have spent applying to different jobs have finally paid off and now you have gotten one foot in the door just by being asked to attend a job interview. Once you have the interview set, what is the next thing you do? Prepare yourself for it of course.

During any interview you will only have approximately 20-25 minutes to tell your interviewers all about your previous work experiences, what skills you have and what kind of person you are as a whole. While this may seem overwhelming, there are a few helpful tips that you can follow to help you succeed in wowing your interviewers. In this chapter we will go into detail about everything you need to know about the interview process and what are several things you can do to help you nail your interview the first time.

What You Need To Do Prior To your Interview

There are a variety of different things that you should do before walking through the door towards your interview. These things can mean the difference between wowing your interviewer and turning them off to the idea of you working for their company. Here is a list of small things you can do to help you succeed during your interview.

1. Do Some Research-In order to know exactly what kind of company you could potentially be working for, it is important to find out a little more about the company first. There are a number of ways that you can do this: either visit the company's location in person or visit the company's website if they have one available. Find out what kind of services or products they offer to their clients, what kind of people already work there, how many hours you will be asked to work and what will the day-to-day grind be like?

While you conduct your research, on a piece of paper take notes about certain things that you want to ask your potential employer at the end of your interview session, which is actually a good thing to do anyway. By research the company you want to find a job at will help you to stand out about the other interviewees and help get you noticed by the interviewer. This shows the interviewer that you have a genuine interest in working for the company and can help go along way in ensuring you get the position that you want.

2. Practice, practice and practice-while this may seem strange, especially once you start doing it, this can help you go a long way in preparing for your interview. This will help you to sound more clear and concise during the actual interview and may even help you get over your nervousness. During your practice session make a list of important points about yourself that you want to point out and practice answering them while looking at yourself in the bathroom mirror. The reason why it is important that you practice before the interview is because this will help you from straying off during the process and sounding unpolished. This will also give you the chance to actually discover what it is that makes you the most ideal candidate for the position you are applying for.

3. Make Sure That You Dress For The Part-remember, your interviewer's will judge you based upon their first impression of you. To help ensure that you impress your interviewer right from the get-go make sure that you dress well for the interview. Remember, it is always a good idea to dress more professional than the other people that are working there. For example, if you are applying for a job as a nurse or veterinary technician, do not come to your interview dressed in scrubs unless it is for a working interview at a hospital. Instead come dressed a dark conservative suit. This applies to both men and women. For men make sure that you wear a collared shirt and a nice tie. For women it is important that you avoid wearing excessive perfume or jewelry. Also for both parties make sure that you are well groomed before hand as nothing will turn an employer off more than a messy head of hair.

If you are not sure what to wear to your interview it is always safer to dress more conservatively and professionally. It is always better to come to an interview overdressed than underdressed. Dressing professionally will give the interviewer a general idea of how professional you are and how dedicated you are to getting the job that you want.

4. Make Sure That You Keep Good Etiquette During The Entire Interview-if I were to write about the thousands of do's and don'ts of what should happen during an interview, this book would truly be over a million pages long. However, there are some basic etiquette guidelines that you should keep in mind such as showing up for your interview on time or preferably early, being aware of your body language and keep the entire interview as positive as possible.

I cannot stress enough how important it is to show up on time for your interview. Not only will your interviewer expect this, but it will be expected of you the moment you are hired. If you show up late to your interview, your interviewer will see a person that will potentially have trouble getting to work on time or may have difficulty meeting their deadlines. If you show up late, there is a highly probable chance that you will not be hired.

You need to be aware of your body language as a whole simply because a lot of what you do physically will tell the interviewer a lot about you even if no words are said. So make sure that your handshake is firm but not overly so, keep your posture as straight as possible and try to remain calm throughout the entire interview process. Above all make sure that you do not slouch in your seat. If you do the interviewer may have the perception that you are bored and uninterested in whatever he or she is saying. When you speak only be polite and courteous. Use proper sentence structure and avoid using any slang words.

When it comes to keeping the entire interview process positive, what I mean is to avoid making any negative remarks about any of the previous jobs or employers that you may have had. Also try to only say positive things about any job-related tasks and responsibilities that the interviewers may ask you. Remember, interviewers look to hire only positive people to work for their company. The need someone who will be willing to tackle challenges head on all while maintaining a positive attitude.

5. Be Prepared With Your Own List of Questions-this is the part of the interview process where the research you conducted earlier will come into play. Remember, potential employers will be looking to hire people that show a true interest in the position they are hiring for so asking a bunch of questions about the company and the work that will be involved is a great way to help you stand above the rest of the candidates out there. This is also the chance where you can ask a variety of your own questions such as what the position is about, what are the time requirements that will be expected of you and what is the company looking for from the person who will be filling in the position.

6. Don't Forget To Send A Thank You Note-once the interview is complete don't forget to thank the interviewer for taking the time to meet with you. Once you get home immediately send the interview or employee a thank you note stating the same thing. The reason that you want to do this is not only because it is proper interviewing etiquette, but it will also help to leave a positive impression on the employer.

The Most Common Interviewing Mistakes That You Should Avoid Making

Have you ever wondered what are the things you should avoid doing during any interview that you have? You would not be the only one so I have come up with a list of the most common mistakes any person can make during the interview process. Read through this list carefully and spend the time necessary that you can avoid making these mistakes in the future.

1. Not Preparing Prior To The Interview- if you cannot answer the simple question, "What is it that you know about this company?" You will be in big trouble during the interview. It is important to get as much background information on the company you are applying to such as the company's history, where it is located and its mission statement. As I said before, this will show your interviewer that you are truly interested in whatever position you are applying for and will show that you have an actual interest in the company.

Make sure that you review all of this information ahead of time and try to commit it to your memory. Also if the company you are applying to has a current Facebook or LinkedIn social profile, it is worth it to take the time to check these out too.

2. Not Dressing For The Part-when it comes to dressing correctly for an interview, you need to be aware of the position you are applying for so that you know exactly how to come dressed to the interview. For example, if you are applying for a professional position in a large company I recommend dressing in professional attire such as a business suit or business dress. If you are applying to a job at a water resort, then I would recommend dressing in something a bit more casual.

If you do not know what to wear to your interview I highly recommend that you scope out the company first hand and see what kind of clothes the employees are wearing. Notice what they are wearing and plan on dressing better than them.

3. Having Poor Communication Skills-I cannot express how important it is to talk with everyone you meet and see on your quest to find a new job. It is just as important to stay connected to every person in a positive way. It is important that you make sure that you shake hands with whoever you may meet, sound confident when you speaks and let them know why you believe you would make a great candidate for the position you are applying for. You should do this right before the actual interview even begins.

4. Bring Useless Objects With You To The Interview-there is absolutely no need for you to bring your cell phone, coffee or any food with you during your interview. Having these objects in the interviewers visibility range will show them that you are unprofessional and not the right candidate for the job. The only things that you should bring with you to an interview if your resume, a list of references, a cover letter (if you wish) and the actual application you filled out.

5. Talking A Little Too Much-one of the things that I hated whenever I was interviewing people for my company was a person who didn't know when to shut their mouth and just went on and on. Look, it is not important for the job for the interviewer to learn your entire life story. Keep in mind that you should always answer whatever questions the interviewer may have for you in a focused manner and make sure that you get straight to the point. Don't ramble on about something completely irrelevant for five minutes. This will certainly not get you the job that you want.

6. Not Talking Enough-Yes there is such a thing as not talking enough during an interview. Remember, the whole point of an interview is for your potential employer to get to know you better and hear straight from you why you would make an excellent candidate for the position they are hiring for. You want to make sure that you answer questions with more than a word or two. Answer any questions the interviewer may throw at you with as much detail as you can without saying too much.

7. Make Sure All Of Your Facts Are The Same Every Time-there is nothing more annoying than having a person you are interviewing that has both a resume and a job application that has to different kinds of dates and information on them. When you apply for a job, chances are that you will need to fill out an application on top of submitting your resume. You need to make sure that all of the dates and contact information matches on both sets so your potential employer can see how consistent you are with your information.

8. Answering the Questions Incorrectly- this is something that can make or break your interview in a heartbeat. To answer all of your interviewer's questions correctly make sure that you listen to every question as hard as you can and take a moment to gather your own thoughts prior to answering. Answering incorrectly will not land you the job. It will only prolong your unemployment period.

9. Talking Trash About Your Past Jobs-if you make the mistake of badmouthing your past jobs or employers I can assure you that you will never be called in for a second interview let alone be hired. If you make the remark that everybody you worked for were idiots or that your boss was a jerk, do you honestly think that an interviewer is going to give you a job right on the spot when you could potentially talk trash about their company?

You may be surprised how small of a world we truly live in. If you bad mouth a previous company that you worked for, you may be in for a shock if it turns out that your interviewer knows your old boss on a personal level. Morale of the story, only say things that are positive no matter if it is not necessarily true.

10. Forgetting To Follow Up With your Interviewer-If you are unsure if you made a positive impression or aren't sure if you aced your interview, the best thing that you can do is to follow up with your interviewer. Regardless of how you did at the interview make sure that you send a thank you not to your interviewer, letting them know that you are grateful that they took time out of their busy schedule in order to meet with you and make sure that you remind the interviewer of your continued interest in the position.

Remember, it is ok if you completely fail at an interview. The worst thing that is going to happen is that you need to schedule another interview at another location. If you fail at an interview keep your head up and ask yourself what it was that you messed up on. Remember, practice makes

Chapter Three: How To Successfully Nail Your Interview

If you are facing a pending job interview you will need to be as prepared as possible so that you can successfully nail it and to claim the job that you want. In this chapter we will go through a few helpful tips that you can use to help ensure that you get the job of your dreams and to wow your potential employer.

Helpful Steps To Follow To Help You Ace Your Interview

Step One: Analyze The Job First

One of the most important things that you can do before the interview itself is to make sure that you analyze every aspect of the job you are applying for. You don't want to apply for a computer programming job if you know absolutely nothing computers as a whole. This is usually easily to find, as many job listings will include every detail of what kind of person the company is looking for.

Once you have that important detail, make sure that you write down a list comprising of your own unique skills whether they are professional or personal and make sure that they are exactly what the company is looking for. If they aren't then I would recommend applying for another position instead.

Step Two: Make Sure That Your Own Qualifications Match Whatever It Is The Company Is Looking For

When you made your list in the previous step, I recommended that you make a list of both your professional and personal attributes. In this step what I am asking you to do is make a list of your professional attributes only. For example, if you are applying for a nursing position it is important to note where you went to school, where you did your internship at and what kind of surgeries you have participated in if there are any. If you are applying for a computer programming position it will be important to note how many years of experience you have in using HTML, C++ or any other previous computer programming experience that you may have.

When you create your list not only should you list what kind of skills you have, but also note any certifications you have received or professional experiences you may have had. Once you list these it will give both you and your potential employer an idea if you are going to be the perfect person for the position.

Prior to the interview make sure that you review the list you have created and commit them to memory that way you can easily answer any question right away the moment an interviewer may ask them.

Step Three: Look Up The Company Beforehand

I cannot express this enough: it is extremely important to learn more about the company that you are applying to prior to walking into your interview. Not only will this help to show that you are truly interested in the position, but it will also help to give you an idea of the type of questions an interviewer may ask you. By researching the company prior to the interview will also give you an idea if the company and the overall work culture will be the best fit for you in the long run.

This will only take a few minutes or up to an hour or two at most for you to do. Again if the company has an active social media profile and you can check out, I recommend that you do so.

Social media profiles such as a Twitter, Facebook or LinkedIn account will give you an in depth idea of what the company stands for and what it plans to achieve with their clients.

Step Four: Practice Your Interview The Night Before

You will never regret practicing for your interview the night before you actually have to do it in front of a real interviewer. This will give you an opportunity to think of good responses to the variety of questions an interviewer may ask of you and will help you to remain calm during the entire process.

You can easily practice for your interview with a close friend or a family member. It is a good idea to review some questions with them that you may have not heard of before and make sure to jot down whatever criticism they may give you.

Here are a couple of questions that you may encounter during your interview so make sure that you come up with your own unique answer beforehand and make sure that you practice answering enough times that you end up memorizing what it is that you want to say.

Questions About Your Personal Work History

1. What were your responsibilities at your previous place of employment?

2. What challenges did you face on a day-to-day basis? If there were any, how did you handle them?

3. Was there anything you liked or disliked about your previous job?

4. Was there anything that you have learned from any mistakes that you may have made?

Questions Just About You

1. What do you consider to be your greatest weakness?

2. What do you consider to be your greatest strength?

3. Do you ever take your work home with you?

4. Do you work well with the people around you?

5. How do you deal with stress?

Questions Pertaining To Money

1. What is your salary expectation?

2. If you have salary requirements what would they be both for the short-term and the long-term?

Questions About Your Job Qualifications

1. Do you think you are overqualified for this job? If so, why?

2. What experience do you have that is relevant to this job?

3. Have you ever had a problem with an employee? If so, how did you handle it?

Questions Regarding The Company

1. What interested you in applying for this job?

2. Why do you want this job in the first place?

3. Give us a reason as to why we should hire you?

4. What can you bring to this company?

Questions About Your Future

1. What career goals do you have? If you have any, how do you plan to reach those goals?

2. If we hire you, how do you feel about being managed by a person that is younger than you?

Step Five: Pick Out your Clothes You Will Be Wearing To The Interview The Night Before

I highly recommend that you don't wait until the day of your interview to prepare whatever it is that you plan to wear. You will be under too much stress as it is to really put some thought and consideration behind the kind of outfit you will need to wear in order to impress your interviewer. I highly recommend that you have an outfit specifically for interviews and have it set aside at all times simply because you never know when you are going to need it.

Remember, regardless of what kind of job you are applying for, it is important to make a great first impression right from the start. Also dress for the position you are applying for and always dress for the job that you want. If you are applying for a business position at a corporate office, then make sure to wear professional attire. If you are applying for a job in a more casual setting then you can wear something a bit more casual but make sure that your outfit is both tidy and well groomed prior to the actual interview.

Step Six: Bring All Of Your Important Documents To Your Interview With You

There are certain things that you will need to bring to your interview. Some of these things include a work portfolio if you have one and if one is needed, make sure to bring your resume so that your interviewer can see it or so that you can reference it later, a list of professional reference and a list of questions about the company and the position if you have any.

It is imperative that you do not bring your cell phone, a cup of coffee or a pack of chewing gum with you as this will look unprofessional to your interviewer and you will most likely not get the job that you want.

Step Seven: Interview Etiquette

You need to keep in mind that having etiquette during your interview is just as important as anything else that will be required during your interview. Knowing this, do not forget to greet the receptionist if there is one at the front desk, greet everyone you come across as politely as you can and be as enthusiastic as you can during the interview process without overdoing it.

Remember to lean forward towards your interviewer, as this will give the idea that you are truly interested in the position. If you look too relaxed or too casual, the interviewer may think that you are uninterested in the position. It is important to show that you want the job you are interviewing for and that you are the most ideal candidate for the position.

Keep in mind that the more of a positive impression that you leave on your interviewer, the better the overall interview will go.

Step Eight: Make Sure You Know How To Get To Your Interview Beforehand

There is nothing worse than showing up to your interview late simply because you got lost along the way. If you have a GPS in your car then make sure that you put it to good use. If you don't then simply hop onto Google Maps and get the directions that you need. I always recommend that you take a trip to the place where your interview is going to be held at the day before, so that you know exactly where it is that you need to go.

Remember, the day of your interview, make sure that you give yourself adequate time to get to the place and take into consideration any construction or traffic that you may run in to along the way. It is always better to show up to an interview early rather than showing up late.

Step Nine: Listen Carefully During The Entire Interview

During your job interview, it is just as important to listen as much as you can then answering the questions correctly. To give you an idea on how important it is, what happens if your interviewer asks you a question and you haven't been paying attention? How will you know what kind of answer they are looking for? You won't and if you answer the question incorrectly it could mean the loss of a potential job.

It is extremely important that you listen to your interviewer the entire time, pay attention to whatever it is he or she is saying and make sure that you take the time necessary to gather your thoughts before answering any question.

Besides listening carefully to your interviewer, you need to be ready to engage your interviewer as well. What I mean is that you want to make sure that you are ready to make friendly conversation with this person so that you can begin building a relationship with them. So in order to do this make sure that you have a few questions of your own to ask the interviewer.

At the end of the interview make sure that you let the interviewer know what your thoughts are about the position. Suck up to them in other words and make sure that you tell them that you are very interested in the position and why you think you would make the best candidate.

Step Ten: Don't Forget To Follow Up

By following at the end of a job interview let's the interviewer know that you are truly interested in the position and let's them know that they should consider you for the position.

Think of a follow up card or letter as a follow up sales letter. You are reinstating why you are the best person for the position, why you want the job so badly, why you are qualified for the position and how you would help the company reach its long term goals. Remember, you want to leave a lasting impression and nothing does it better than a follow up letter.

A Few Things To Do and Not Do During Your Interview

To wrap up this eBook in this section we will go through a few things that you should and shouldn't do during your interview. The reason that I want to touch on these points is simply because there are many people out there that simply don't know what to do in an interview and I want to help you to prevent making crucial mistakes that will certainly not help you get the job that you want.

What You Want To Do In An Interview

1. Make sure that you dress appropriately for your interview regardless of the position you are applying for. Also make sure that you are very well groomed and look presentable for the interview.

2. Make sure that you know the exact time and place where your interview is going to be held. Note how long it will take you to get to that place and make sure that you give yourself enough time to arrive early. Also make sure to account for any construction or traffic that you may come across along the way.

3. Always try to arrive to your interview about 10-15 minutes early. Sometimes a potential employer will tell you to do so anyway.

4. Remember to greet every person that you come across in a friendly and courteous

manner. The people that you greet will voice their opinions of you to the employer and may affect the outcome of whether or not you will be hired for the position.

5. When shaking hands with your interviewer, shake it with a firm and steady grip. During the handshake make eye contact and smile brightly as this will give the interviewer a good first impression of you right off the bat.

6. Memorize your interviewer's name and until they say to do otherwise always speak to them while using the title Miss or Mister.

7. Make eye contact every couple of seconds or so. This will let the interviewer know that you are paying full attention to every word they are saying.

8. Sit completely still in your seat even if you are very nervous.

9. When answering questions make sure that

you take time to think about your answer before you respond. When you do answer don't forget to give specific example to give your interviewer the chance to understand your statement.

10. Remain honest when answering these question and make sure that you keep a professional attitude the entire time.

What Not To Do In Your Interview

1. Never make excuses for yourself. Remain accountable for any past actions or mistakes that you have made in your professional career.

2. Don't treat the interview itself as a casual moment and don't talk to your interviewer like he or she is your friend. This is a professional moment and you will be judge on how professional you may or may not be.

3. Don't practice for your interview the night before. It is paramount that you practice for the interview the day before so you can be ready to answer any questions the interviewer may throw at you.

4. Don't come into an interview chewing gum or reeking of cigarette smoke.

5. Do not make any negative statements or comments about a past job or past employer that you may have had. Always remain positive throughout the entire interview process.

6. Don't lie on your application or your resume. Dishonesty is one thing that all employers do not tolerate and it can easily be discovered if you falsified any documents that you may have filled out.

7. Don't let your cell phone to ring during the interview. Turn it out or put it on silent. If you let it ring it will look very unprofessional to your interviewer.

8. Do not let your interviewers think that the only reason you are applying for the position is because of the pay that will be given. You need to tell them that you are interested in the position and working long-term with the company or else you certainly will not be hired.

9. Do not become frustrated during the interview. I know looking for a job can be a stressful time but you only want the interviewer to get the impression that you are a usually upbeat and positive person.

10. Don't slouch in your set. This will give the impression that you are bored with the entire interview and that you are not serious about the position whatsoever.

Conclusion

When it comes to preparing for your next job interview, there is no need to stress yourself about the entire process. The key to nailing your interview is to prepare, prepare and to prepare some more. The interview is the first step into working for a company that you may have wanted to work for some time and it is the only thing standing between you and the job of your dreams.

Remember, all you have to really do is to prepare for the interview the night before whether that is practicing answering the different questions an interviewer may ask you, picking out the outfit you plan on wearing to the interview, getting directions to the place of the interview or memorizing every aspect of your resume and job application. For some people passing a job interview is one of the hardest obstacles to overcome while for others they look forward to the challenge and feel confident that they can do it.

Regardless of what category you fit into, I have no doubt that after reading this eBook that you will be able to do so as well. Remember, remain calm and practice as much as you can. With the right preparation and attitude you can easily overcome the interview and grab the dream job you have always wanted.

About Us

The Thought Flame is committed to add value to its customers through various books, online courses and other resources. You can learn more about us and our books at www.thethoughtflame.com.

Don't forget to check out our amazing **online video courses** at www.thethoughtflame.com/courses/ to take your knowledge to another level.

To check out our **extraordinary collection of diet/cookbooks**, visit http://www.thethoughtflame.com/category/non-fictional/cookbooks/ .

As a part of our valued relationship with our customers, we keep providing you free promotional books, courses and other stuff on subscribing with us on our site. We have a strict anti-spam policy and assure you no spam mails will be sent to your mailbox.

To subscribe with us, visit

www.thethoughtflame.com.

Like our work and would like to say thanks?

Buy us a cup of coffee at

www.thethoughtflame.com/coffee/

__Author__

Amarpreet Singh is an avid learner and his passion for education has made him travel, work and study all across the world. He holds three masters degrees, including MBA, from top universities in Asia.

He is author of dozens of books, many of which are Amazon's bestseller, varying in various topics and categories. He also teaches many online courses having thousands of students across the world.

He has a keen interest in international affairs, economics, global poverty and politics, financial markets and entrepreneurship, and strives to be part of a community that shares the same passion.

He has worked as consultant with organizations like Airbus and The World Bank.

He loves travelling and learning about new cultures, and has been fortunate to live/work/travel/study in countries like India, China, Korea, US, South Africa, Japan, Philippines, Singapore, Canada etc., and learn about the culture and lifestyle in each of them.

To check out more of his work, visit www.thethoughtflame.com